797,885 Books
are available to read at

www.ForgottenBooks.com

Forgotten Books' App
Available for mobile, tablet & eReader

ISBN 978-1-330-51865-6
PIBN 10072816

This book is a reproduction of an important historical work. Forgotten Books uses state-of-the-art technology to digitally reconstruct the work, preserving the original format whilst repairing imperfections present in the aged copy. In rare cases, an imperfection in the original, such as a blemish or missing page, may be replicated in our edition. We do, however, repair the vast majority of imperfections successfully; any imperfections that remain are intentionally left to preserve the state of such historical works.

Forgotten Books is a registered trademark of FB &c Ltd.
Copyright © 2017 FB &c Ltd.
FB &c Ltd, Dalton House, 60 Windsor Avenue, London, SW19 2RR.
Company number 08720141. Registered in England and Wales.

For support please visit www.forgottenbooks.com

1 MONTH OF FREE READING

at

www.ForgottenBooks.com

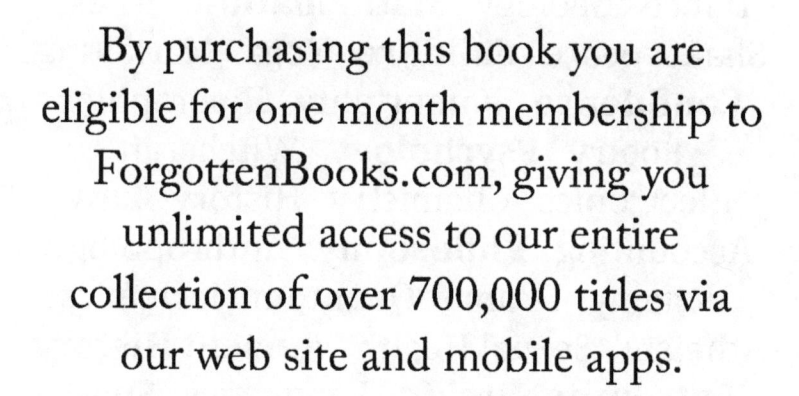

By purchasing this book you are eligible for one month membership to ForgottenBooks.com, giving you unlimited access to our entire collection of over 700,000 titles via our web site and mobile apps.

To claim your free month visit: www.forgottenbooks.com/free72816

* Offer is valid for 45 days from date of purchase. Terms and conditions apply.

English
Français
Deutsche
Italiano
Español
Português

www.forgottenbooks.com

Mythology Photography **Fiction**
Fishing Christianity **Art** Cooking
Essays Buddhism Freemasonry
Medicine **Biology** Music **Ancient Egypt** Evolution Carpentry Physics
Dance Geology **Mathematics** Fitness
Shakespeare **Folklore** Yoga Marketing
Confidence Immortality Biographies
Poetry **Psychology** Witchcraft
Electronics Chemistry History **Law**
Accounting **Philosophy** Anthropology
Alchemy Drama Quantum Mechanics
Atheism Sexual Health **Ancient History**
Entrepreneurship Languages Sport
Paleontology Needlework Islam
Metaphysics Investment Archaeology
Parenting Statistics Criminology
Motivational

SYLLABUS

OF A

COURSE OF LECTURES

ON

BETHAN LITERATURE:—

THE DRAMA.

TO BE DELIVERED

FAX AND BURY ST. EDMUND'S IN THE MICHAELMAS
TERM, 1887,

BY

I. GOLLANCZ, B.A.,

SCHOLAR OF CHRIST'S COLLEGE, CAMBRIDGE.

WERTHEIMER, LEA & CO., CIRCUS PLACE, LONDON WALL.

Cambridge University Extension Lectures.

With sincerest regards
J. G.

SYLLABUS

OF A

COURSE OF LECTURES

ON

ELIZABETHAN LITERATURE:—

THE DRAMA.

TO BE DELIVERED

AT HALIFAX AND BURY ST. EDMUND'S IN THE MICHAELMAS
TERM, 1887,

BY

I. GOLLANCZ, B.A.,

SCHOLAR OF CHRIST'S COLLEGE, CAMBRIDGE.

TEXT BOOKS.—The lecturer recommends as text-books, Morley's *First Sketch of English Literature* (Cassell, 7s. 6d.), to be used with Morley's *Plays* (Cassell, 7s. 6d.), (Library of English Literature), Dowden's *Shakespeare Primer* (Macmillan, 1s.)

Students who have access to libraries may consult throughout the course :—

Ward's *English Dramatic Literature*, Collier's *English Dramatic Poetry*, Symond's *Shakespeare's Predecessors in the English Drama*.

Reference to special books is made at the end of each lecture.

WEEKLY EXAMINATION QUESTIONS.—In order to be admitted to the final examination (on the result of which, combined with that of the class work, the University certificates are awarded), students are required, not only to have attended the lectures and classes, but also to have satisfied the lecturer in at least one half of the weekly papers.

Answers to the weekly examination questions, endorsed with the writer's name or *nom de plume* and centre, should be posted to I. Gollancz, Esq., Christ's College, Cambridge, so as to arrive as follows —:

From the Halifax classes, Tuesday morning.

From the Bury St. Edmund's classes, Tuesday evening.

Papers from Bury St. Edmund's should also be endorsed with the words "Afternoon Class,"—"Evening Class."

LECTURE I.

THE DRAMA AND THE BIBLE-STORY.

A.—INTRODUCTION.
1. During the first thirty years of Elizabeth's reign three classes of playwrights co-existed:—
   (*a*) linked itself to the earlier English drama,
   (*b*) followed classical models,
   (*c*) tried to effect a compromise between (*a*) and (*b*).
2. This is the period of the formation of the drama, its maturity is reached when the compromise sought after by (*c*) is effected; this takes place soon after 1588.
3. The type of the national drama once fixed is brought to perfection by Shakespeare.
4. The earlier plays of the poet reveal the varied influences through which he had to pass before finding the dramatic form best suited to his genius.

To trace the growth of the drama through these different stages, and to demonstrate Shakespeare's relation to the contemporary dramatists is the object of this course of lectures.

B.—THE RELIGIOUS DRAMA.
1. Wherever a dramatic literature has sprung up, it is found in its beginnings associated with religious worship. This is true of the Indian, Egyptian, Chinese, Greek, and also of the modern (*i.e.* Christian) drama.
2. The Modern Drama is to be traced back to—
   i. The liturgical mystery.
   (*a*) The Office of the Mass contained elements essentially dramatic.
   (*b*) The Church very early illustrated the Gospel story by means of tableaux, in order to appeal to the unlettered masses:—
      i. These tableaux were at first merely pantomimic.
      ii. The figures then spoke the story they were to illustrate.

      iii. Special texts were written by the clerics for the performers (about 11th century). These texts were in Latin at first, but were soon in the vernacular (French) in 12th century.

      iv. Not only the Gospel story was thus illustrated, but also the lives of the more popular saints (*e.g.* St. Nicolas).

   ii. The monastic literary drama, *e.g.* Hroswitha's Comedies (10th cent.).

C.—THE RELIGIOUS DRAMA IN ENGLAND.

1. The Religious Drama passed from the Church into the hands of the Guilds, and was developed by them.
2. Religious plays in England were indiscriminately called "miracles;" on the Continent this term was applied only to such as dealt with the legends of the saints, while those dealing with the Scripture-story were called "mysteries."
3. It was the only form of dramatic composition cultivated from the end of the 11th to the middle of the 15th century. No form of intentionally dramatic writing was known in England before the Norman Conquest.

   (*a*) In addition to single plays, four great cycles belonging to this period of collective "Miracle" plays are preserved.

      i. The "Townley" (acted at Woodkirk, near Wakefield).

      ii. The "Chester."

      iii. The "Coventry."

      iv. The "York."

   (*b*) The matter of the "Miracle" plays was drawn from Scripture narrative, modified by apocryphal literature and Biblical legends.

   (*c*) Dramatic elements of the plays.

      i. The Melodramatic character of Herod.

      ii. The Grotesquely-comical character of Lucifer.

      iii. The Pathetic (*e.g.* Sacrifice of Isaac).

      iv. Realistic Comedy.

      v. The Pastoral (*e.g.* the Nativity).

4. Early in the sixteenth century the religious drama widened its range of subjects so as to include secular stories, *e.g. Robert Cicill*, acted at Chester in 1529.
5. During the reign of Elizabeth, Miracle plays continued to be acted,

and during the first ~~seventy~~ years religious plays were written; *five*
the latter "served to mediate between the Catholic mysteries and
the Protestant polemical plays on the one hand, and the artistic
secular drama of the next generation on the other."—(*Herford.*)
  e.g. Enterlude of the story of King Darius (1565).
  Enterlude of godly Queen Hester (1561).
  Play of Susanna (1568), not extant.
  Play on the subject of the Prodigal (1565-6), not extant.
6. Performance of a Miracle play.

QUESTIONS.

1. How far is a study of the Miracle plays a necessary introduction to an understanding of the Elizabethan Drama?
2. Illustrate from English Literature the fact that epic and lyrical poetry develop before dramatic.
3. Describe the performance of a Miracle play.

For the "Townley" Miracles see Surtees Society's Publications, 1836.

For the "Coventry" and "Chester," the Old Shakespeare Society's Publications, 1841 and 1843.

For the "York" see "The York Mystery Plays," edited by Miss Toulmin Smith, 1883.

LECTURE II.

THE DRAMA OF ALLEGORY.

MORALITY PLAYS.

1. "A moral, or moral-play is a drama, the characters of which are allegorical, abstract or symbolical, and the story of which is intended to convey a lesson for the better conduct of human life."
—*Collier.*
2. This form of drama was not known in England before the middle of the fifteenth century. It continued to flonrish actively until the beginning of Elizabeth's reign, and existed side by side with the regular drama during the whole of the sixteenth century.
3. Before the fifteenth century allegorical poetry was represented in England by—
   (*a*) Poems of native growth, *e.g., Piers the Plowman.*

    (*b*) Poems based on foreign models, or due to foreign influence, *e.g.* Chaucer and Gower's poetry.

  The allegorical drama in its origin belonged to the same influences as produced (*b*).

  The allegorical characters found occasionally in the earlier Miracle plays formed no essential part of the plays.

4. Gains to the drama from moralities :—
   (1) Ingenuity of plot necessitated by allegorical form.
   (2) The gradual evolution of real characters due to abstract personification.
   (3) It becomes a mirror of history :—
      i. Old faith plays—*Castle of Perseverance* (reign of Henry VI.).
         Interlude of Youth (about 1555).
      ii. Reformation Plays—*Lusty Juventus* (about 1550).
         New Custom (pr. 1573).
      iii. Conflict between i. and ii., seen in *Conflict of Conscience* (pr. 1581).
      iv. Plays of the New Science—*Nature of the Four Elements* (1517-19).
      v. Plays of the New Learning—*The Trial of Treasure* (pr. 1567).

5. Morality plays, like the Miracles, satisfied popular taste by means of
   (1) Comic scenes, introduced merely to relieve monotony of action.
   (2) Comic characters—the Devil,
      the Vice (a character peculiar to the Moralities).

6. The introduction of real personages into the Moral plays gradually led to the displacement of the allegorical characters.
   The two elements co-exist in—
      i. Comedy— { *Tom Tiler and his wife* (about 1569).
         Morality { *Jack Juggler* (Edward VI.)
      ii. Tragedy— { *Apius and Virginia* (about 1563).
         Morality { *King Cambises* (1561 ?).
      iii. History—Bale's *Kynge Johan* (about 1548).
         Morality.

7. John Heywood's *Interludes*, in which allegorical characters no longer appear, hold a middle place between moralities and regular drama :—
      i. *The Mery Play between Johan Johan the Husband, Tyb his Wife, and Sir Ihan the Priest*, printed 1533.

ii. *The Four P's* (the Palmer, the Pardoner, the 'Poticary, and the Pedlar), about 1540.

　　iii. *The Mery Play between the Pardoner and the Frere*, printed 1533, written before 1521.

8. The development of the "Interlude" into regular comedy is seen in *Gammer Gurton's Needle*; this play was long regarded as our earliest English comedy (it was performed at Christ's College, Cambridge, in 1566).

9. While the farcical elements of the "Moralities" led to regular comedy, the allegorical lived on in the Masque.

QUESTIONS.

1. How far is it just to regard the Morality as developed from the Miracle Plays?
2. Compare Skelton's *Morality of Magnificence* and Lyndsay's *Satire of Three Estates*.
3. Trace the development of comedy and history from the Morality plays.

The text of most of the plays mentioned are printed in Dodsley's Old English plays.

LECTURE III.

THE LATIN DRAMA IN ENGLAND.

A.—CLASSICAL MODELS.

1. The living interest in classical antiquity, characteristic of the Renaissance, was fully represented in Elizabethan literature. Its influence on the English Drama may be broadly summed up under four heads:—
　　i. In the choice of classical models;
　　ii. In the choice of subjects drawn from classical mythology;
　　iii. In the use of classical allusions as part of dramatic diction;
　　iv. In the introduction of classical machinery outside the main action of the drama.
2. Of these influences i. was of most importance in its effects on dramatic art.
3. It must be borne in mind that it was the Latin Drama and not the Greek which influenced the Renaissance drama:—

i. Seneca (1st cent. A.D.) was regarded as the model for tragedy;
   ii. Plautus and Terence (2nd cent. B.C.) for comedy.
      (Observe that between 1559 and 1581 "Seneca, his tenne Tragedies" were translated into English.)

4. These writers became the model on which the first regular English comedies and tragedies were based:—
   i. *Ralph Roister Doister* (1551 or earlier);
   ii. *Gorboduc*, (1592).

5. Both plays may be described as academic plays, *i.e.*, intended for select audiences.

6. The acting of plays as an academic exercise was a regular institution in England from the first quarter of the 16th century. These were as a general rule in Latin. Occasionally, however, English was allowed. To this concession we owe *Ralph Roister Doister*.

7. Aided by Italian example, the English playwrights of the classical school were not slavish imitators of their masters. At the outset they chose for their subjects episodes dealing with English life or national legend.
   (Towards the close of the century we find a few exotic examples of real Senecan plays, such are:— Kyd's *Cornelia*, 1594, translated from the French, Daniel's *Cleopatra*, and *Philotus*, 1594.)

B.—RALPH ROISTER DOISTER:—
   i. Its author   — Nicholas Udall, Master at Eton and Westminster;
   ii. Its occasion   — Probably written for the Christmas performance held annually at Eton;
   iii. Source   — Miles Gloriosus of Plautus;
   iv. The extant text — The unique copy of this play, discovered in 1818, has no title-page, but it was certainly printed in Elizabeth's reign; the prayer at the end can be for no other than Elizabeth;
   v. Classical influence— In construction of the plot and in the arrangement of the play into five acts.
   vi. Native elements:—
      (*a*) In the choice of story dealing with English life;
      (*b*) In *dramatis personæ*.
         These are real English characters, both in name and

action. The "vice" of the morality and the parasite of classical comedy are blended in *Matthew Merrygreek*. Note the alliterated names:—*Ralph Roister Doister, Christian Cunstance, Madge Mumblecheek, Tibet Talkapace, Dobinet Doughty*, etc.

  (*c*) In its diction.

C.—GORBODUC :—
- i. Its authors— Thomas Sackville, Lord Buckhurst, scholar and statesman, with Thomas Norton ;
- ii. Its occasion—Acted before Elizabeth by the gentlemen of the Inner Temple ;
- iii. It follows Senecan tragedy in—
    - (*a*) Making the action take place behind the scenes ;
    - (*b*) Ending each act with a chorus ;
    - (*c*) Substituting declamation for action and dialogue.
      "It is full of stately speeches and well-sounding phrases, clyming to the height of Seneca his stile, and as full of notable moralities which it doth most delightfully teach."— (Sidney's *Apologie for Poetrie*.)
- iv. It deserts classical example :—
    - (*a*) In neglecting the unities of time and place.
      "It is faulty both in time and place, the two necessary companions of all corporall actions."— (*Sidney*.)
    - (*b*) In its choice of subject ;
    - (*c*) In its use of dumb-show.
- v. It is the first play in which blank verse is used. (For the use of this verse on the ordinary stage, see Lecture VI.)

As similar in construction to *Gorboduc* are to be noted :—

(1) *The Misfortunes of Arthur*, acted before the Queen at Greenwich, in 1587, in which, with others, Lord Bacon (born 1561) had a hand. It is superior to *Gorboduc* in characterisation, diction and versification.

(2) *Tancred and Gismunda* (first acted 1568), the oldest English play extant, founded on an Italian novel.—Originally written in rhyme by gentlemen of the Inner Temple, where it was acted before the Queen.—Republished in 1592 (see Lecture VI.), "polished according to the decorum of these days," *i.e.*, put into blank verse. In the last act the romantic character of the subject triumphs over the writer's classicism, and, contrary to classical example, Gismunda and her father die on the stage.

D.—Gascoigne's "Glasse of Government" (about 1575).
> (1) This comedy stands alone among English Elizabethan plays in its attempt "to connect *Terentian situations* with a *Christian moral* in a picture of school life."
> (2) It is due to the German Latin "school-dramas" of the early part of the sixteenth century in which the parable of the Prodigal Son was "classicised."

To the influence of Germany, too, is due a series of sacred pre-Elizabethan Latin dramas. These stand for the most part outside the history of the popular drama. It has, however, lately been shown that to one of the most important of these (Pammachius), Bale's *Kynge Johan*, owes much, and that it was this imitation which "finally emancipated Bale from his clumsy efforts to build a Protestant drama on the ruins of the Catholic mystery" (see Herford's "The Literary Relation of England and Germany in the Sixteenth Century").

Questions.

1. Write a short Essay on the Renaissance in its relation to the beginnings of the English drama.
2. What is understood by the "Unities"?
   Give the substance of and criticise Sidney's opinion on *Gorboduc* and its defects.
3. *Ralph Roister Doister* and *Gammer Gurton's Needle* hold different places in the history of the drama. Explain this.

Ralph Roister Doister is printed among Arber's Reprints (price 6d.) On Latin plays see C. H. Herford's Studies on "the Literary Relations of England and Germany in the Sixteenth Century," chap. iii.

LECTURE IV.

THE TWILIGHT OF THE ELIZABETHAN DRAMA.

A.—Italian Influence on the Elizabethan Drama.
> 1. It has already been mentioned that the influence of the classical drama was due to the example of Italy. But a more direct influence

of Italy is observed in that species of the drama which combined the characteristics of the classical school on the one hand, and of the popular drama on the other. This, the "romantic" drama, is entirely due to Italian influence. Probably two-thirds of the Elizabethan dramas may be traced to Italian sources. This is not remarkable when the influences of Italian on English literature in the sixteenth century are passed in review.

2. General influences of Italian on English literature in the sixteenth century.

   i. "In the latter end of the same King's reigne (Henry VIII.) sprŏg vp a new companie of courtly makers, of whom Sir Thomas Wyat the elder, and Henry, Earle of Surrey, were the two chieftains, who having trauelled to Italie, and there tasted the sweete and stately measures and stile of the Italian Poesie, as novices newly crept out of the schooles of Dante, Ariosto, and Petrarch, they greatly pollished our rude and homely mañer of vulgar poesie from that it had bene before, and for that cause may iustly be sayd the first reformers of our English meetre and stile."—Puttenham, "Art of English Poesie." 1589.

   Their services were :—
   - (*a*) Introduction of the Sonnet.
   - (*b*) Introduction of blank verse.
   - (*c*) Refinement of English Diction.

   (See Tottle's *Miscellany*.)

   ii. Novel literature :—
   - 1562. Rhymed English version of some of Boccaccio's tales.
   - 1562. Brooke's verse paraphrases of Bandello's story of *Romeus and Julietta*.
   - 1565. Translation of Ariosto's *Ariodanto and Ginevra*.
   - 1566. Sixty novels from Boccaccio :—Painter's *Palace of Pleasure*.
   - 1567. Thirty-four novels from Bandello and Cinthio, &c., &c.
   - 1583. Belleforest's Repository.

   Ascham, in *The Schoolmaster* (1570), protests against the evils caused by these owing to their indecency.

   iii. On the language.

   Italian terms quite common, many of them naturalized, *e.g*, sonnet, madrigal, umbrella, motto, &c.

    iv. On epic poetry. This influence is strong towards the end of the century :—" Spenser," to quote Gabriel Harvey, " overgoes the *Orlando Furioso*, in his *Elfish Queen*."
        1591. Harrington's translations of *Orlando Furioso*.
        1501. Carew translates five cantos of *Jerusalem Delivered*.
        1600. Fairfax translates the whole poem.

3. General survey of Italian influence on the drama before 1580 :—
    i. The direct influence mentioned above. Notice Gascoigne's *Supposes* and *Jocasta*, both from Italian plays.
    ii. In providing the material for the drama (the novel literature).
        1568. Earliest known play derived from an Italian novel *Tancred and Gismunda*, though Brook (1562) says he had seen the argument of *Romeus and Julietta* set forth.
    iii. In 1578 a company of Italian players came to England to perform before the Queen. Their "extemporal" playing is alluded to by contemporary dramatists.

B.—THE ANNALS OF THE STAGE :—
1. Of the plays produced between 1558 and 1586, comparatively few were printed. It is questionable whether any of the plays written solely for the masses are extant. From contemporary criticism it is clear that these plays linked themselves, in form, to the earlier drama, in subject, to the romantic novels. "I may boldly say it, because I have seen it, that *The Palace of Pleasure*, *The Golden Ass*, *The Æthiopean History*, *Amadis of France*, and *The Round Table*, comedies in Latin, French, Italian, and Spanish have been thoroughly raked to furnish the playhouses in London."—(Gosson, *School of Abuse*, 1579.)
2. Of a list of fifty-two plays acted at Court between 1568 and 1580, eighteen bear antique titles, twenty-one seem founded upon modern history, romances, and stories of a more general kind, seven are comedies, and six morals. None of these plays survive. The plays of this period sent to press were the work rather of amateurs in dramatic art than of professional play-wrights. The plays of the latter were guarded as theatrical property.

C.—BEGINNINGS OF THE "ROMANTIC" DRAMA (1560-1580).
1. During this period the school of playwrights flourished which created the "romantic" drama.
2. Its purpose was to bridge the gap which divided the artless playhouse drama and the artificial classical drama of the *Gorboduc* type :—

i. From the former they borrowed :—
   (*a*) The blending of comedy and tragedy,
   (*b*) Realism,
   (*c*) Rhyming verse.
ii. They were under the influence of the former in :—
   (*a*) Diction,
   (*b*) Dramatic construction,
   (*c*) Method of arrangement of plot.
iii. The best examples of early "Romantic" drama are :—
   Edward's *Damon and Pythias* (printed 1571).
   Whetstone's *Promus and Cassandra* (printed 1578).

D.—THE STATE OF THE DRAMA DURING THE PERIOD MAY BE GATHERED FROM :
1. The external history of the theatre.
   1574. First royal licence to play given to the Earl of Leicester and opposed by the City of London.
   1576. First regular theatres established, "The Theatre," "The Curtain," and "Blackfriars."
2. Contemporary criticism :—
   Whetstone's Dedication to *Promus and Cassandra*.
   Gosson's *School of Abuse*, and connected literature.
   Sidney's *Apologie for Poetrie*.
   Stubb's *Anatomy of Abuses*.

QUESTIONS.

1. What is understood by the "Romantic" drama? Contrast it with the Classical.
2. The extant plays belonging to the period from 1560-1580 are the compositions of "gentlemen-scholars" rather than professional playwrights. Verify this fact and comment on it.
3. Give an account of Gosson's *School of Abuse*, and discuss its place in Elizabethan literary history.

See Arber's Reprints for :—
   Sidney's *Apologie for Poetrie*, and
   Cosson's *School of Abuse*.

LECTURE V.

THE COURTLY DRAMA OF EUPHUISM.

A.—EUPHUES, THE ANATOMY OF WIT, 1578. EUPHUES AND HIS ENGLAND, 1580.

1. The Romances of mediæval Europe had lost their charm by the Sixteenth Century. Lyly wrote his *Euphues* to supply the want of a new form of story-book. Hence its success. It was intended as a book for ladies :—"*Euphues* had rather lie shut in a Ladyes casket, then open in a Schollers studie."

2. Lyly was not the inventor of Euphuism. Two years before the publication of *Euphues*, appeared *A Petite Palace of Pettie his Pleasure*, by George Pettie.

   "Euphuism is only one of the many exaggerations and eccentricities produced by the revival of classical literature. The term is often and was often used to express all the affectations in speech, style, and diction of the Elizabethan age in general."—(*Landmann.*)

3. The history of Euphuism.
   i. It was invented by a Spanish writer, Don Antonio de Guevara, born at the beginning of the sixteenth century. His books were translated into all the chief European languages.
      1529. His *Marco Aurelio* appeared.
      1532. Translated into English by Bourchier, Lord Berners; passed through twelve editions; and also by Sir Thomas North.
      1557. North translates into English *The Dial of the Princes*, and soon after his other works were translated.

   The popularity of Guevara in England may be inferred from the fact that six different translators rendered his works into English during forty years. All the important characteristics of Euphuism are found in Guevara's style, except alliteration. This is explained by the fact that in the "romance" languages it does not exist as in the Teutonic, where it stood in early poetry for rhyme.

4. The subject of *Euphues*, its characteristics and style.
   i. The name "Euphues" is borrowed from Ascham. "It is the first of the 'seven plain notes' whereby Ascham, following Plato, would choose a good wit in a child for learning.

'Euphues' is he that is apt by goodness of wit, and appliable by readiness of will, to learning, having all other qualities of the mind and parts of the body, that must another day serve learning."

ii. The two parts of *Euphues* may be described as a didactic story threading a series of essays on true love and education.

iii. The characteristics of Lyly's style must be, and can be, easily distinguished :—

(a) His *metaphors* are in most instances not exaggerated or affected. His words are genuine English. His ideas sound and reasonable.

(b) The *artificiality* of his style is in the grammatical structure and syntax.

"We have here the most elaborate antithesis, not only of well-balanced sentences, but also of words, often even of syllables."—(*Landmann.*)

(c) *Twin phrases* in juxtaposition or antithesis.

(d) Principal and subordinate phrases opposing one another.

(e) *Alliteration*, consonants, rhyme, playing on words.

(f) *Similes* drawn—

(i.) from classical mythology :

(ii.) from Pliny's fabulous natural history—Lyly's "Unnatural Natural Philosophy."

5. Euphuism reflected in Lyly's plays revealed the brilliancy of which prose dialogue was capable.

B.—LYLY'S PLAYS.

1. They were written for a performance at Court. Like his prose romance, they were a new species of composition. "The lyre he played on had no borrowed strings."—(*Blount*, in the edition of his six Court Comedies, 1632) :—

The Woman in the Moon, before 1584; a simple pastoral comedy. The defects of Lyly's typical style did not appear in this play; unlike the rest of his comedies, it is written in blank verse.

Mother Bombie, printed 1594; a love comedy of "Errors." (Performed about 1584-89.)

Campaspe, printed 1584;

Sappho and Phao, printed 1584;

Endymion, printed 1591. (Performed between 1584-89.)
   The most important of Lyly's plays, "deriving life, or the semblance of life from the reference it unmistakably betrays to real events and personages."—(*Ward*).

Galetea, printed 1592; contains an underplot turning on the disguise of two girls as boys. (Performed about 1589.)

Midas, printed 1592; a political allegory. (Performed between 1584-1589.)

2. General characteristics of Lyly's plays :—
   i. They may be described as comedies founded on classical fable idyllically represented with an allegorical purpose.
   ii. They betray an absence of local colour; the charm of the pastoral form adopted consists in the lyrics interspersed, though these have for the most part nothing to do with the action of the play.

C.—THE NEW ELEMENTS INTRODUCED INTO THE DRAMA BY LYLY :—
   i. Prose dialogue; (attempted by Gascoigne 1556.)
   ii. Dream dramas;
   iii. Disguise of sex;
   iv. The blending of masque and drama.

QUESTIONS.

1. Write a short essay on Euphuism.—Illustrate the influence of the Euphuistic style on the drama.
2. Give a sketch of Lyly's *Endymion;* its form and purpose.
3. Discuss Lyly's place in the history of the drama.

Lyly's Dramatic Works in the Library of Old Authors. 2 vols. (Reeves & Turner, 6s. 6d.)

Euphues has been reprinted by Arber.

The best study of Euphuism is to be found in Landmann's *Euphues, the Anatomy of Wit* (Heilbronn); though published in Germany, the Introduction and Notes are in English. (Price 2s.)

LECTURE VI.

CHRISTOPHER MARLOWE.

Tamberlaine (Parts 1 and 2), written 1585-87, published 1590.
Faustus, written 1587-88 (probably revised later), published 1640.
Jew of Malta, written after 1588, published 1633.
Massacre of Paris (existing only in corrupt condition), 1589, published 1596? (undated).
Edward II., not earlier than 1590, published 1598.
Dido (partly Marlowe's), 1592? published 1594.
Hero and Leander (Sestiads 1 and 2), 1592? published 1598.

A.—GENERAL CHARACTERISTICS OF MARLOWE'S PLAYS.
  1. *Tamberlaine*, Marlowe's first play, marked an epoch in the history of English Drama. Its definite purpose of improving the drama was clearly set forth in its prologue:—

    > "From jigging veins of *rhyming mother* wits
    > And such conceits as clownage keeps in pay
    > We'll lead you to the stately tent of war;
    > Where you shall hear the Scythian Tamburlaine
    > Threatening the world with *high astounding* terms,
    > And scourging kingdoms with his conquering sword."

  2. It affected the compromise between the scholarly classical drama and the popular romantic drama by joining
      (i.) The versification of the former to
      (ii.) The dramatic form of the latter.
  3. To it is due the introduction of blank verse on the popular stage. Before Marlowe's play its use was restricted to plays intended for select audiences. But one feels throughout these plays that in its first stages blank verse was simply unrhymed couplets. The effort of the writers to avoid rhyme is palpable. Marlowe for the first time used blank verse with ease and gave it the freedom of which we know it is capable.
      (i.) Blank verse before *Tamberlaine* used in:—
          (*a*) *Gorboduc*, 1561.
          (*b*) *Jocasta*, 1566.
          (*c*) *Misfortunes of Arthur*, 1587.
          (*d*) *Woman in the Moon*, before 1584.

(ii.) Marlowe's blank verse.

An analytical study of this subject shows clearly that Marlowe had learnt to vary his versification by means of four grea characteristics :—

  (*a*) The use of a trochee for an iambic after a pause in the first, third, and fourth foot.
  (*b*) The use of a certain number of syllables and words which may be long or short, at will.
  (*c*) Extra syllables before a pause.
  (*d*) The introduction of a number of short verses.

(iii.) Evidence of the effect of *Tamberlaine* on versification :—

  (*a*) Plays before 1587 written in rhyme, were, after that date, re-cast in blank verse, *e.g. Tancred and Gismunda, The Three Ladies of London, Selimus.*
  (*b*) Contemporary allusions;—see the Epistle prefixed to Green's *Perimedes*, 1588 ; Nash's Epistle prefixed to Green's *Menaphon*, 1589.

4. Marlowe's type of tragedy.

  (i.) The basis of his drama may be described as the idealisation of gigantic passion on a gigantic scale.
    (*a*) *Tamberlaine* = lust for dominion.
    (*b*) *Barabas* = lust for wealth.
    (*c*) *Faustus* = lust for knowledge.
  (ii.) He had neither the wish nor the power to form a drama of intrigue or character.—Love not used as a motive in any of his plays.—If introduced at all, only as a mere incident.

5. The diction of Marlowe's plays.

  To elevate the dignity of tragedy his terms are all "high astounding." There is an absence of "native mother words." His incongruous use of classical names and allusions was but one of the elements of his grandiloquence. Even more striking is the manner in which his characters speak of themselves in the third person, as though regarding their gigantic personalities from an external standpoint. This objective treatment of character has an heightening effect on his style.

6. The machinery of Marlowe's plays.

  He departed from the popular drama in his sparing use of prologue, epilogue and chorus, and in his avoidance of dumb-show and allegorical figures.

In *Tamberlaine*, for the first time a story was set forth on the stage without the aid of epic chorus of some form or other, or of dumb show.

B.—EDWARD II.

Typical Marlowesque tragedies are :—

Tamberlaine.
Faustus.
Jew of Malta.
} These may be said to constitute Marlowe's first period.

Edward II. must be regarded as the first and only play of what would have been Marlowe's second period. It is distinguished from the first group :—

(i.) In being pitched in a lower key.

(ii.) In power of dramatic characterisation.

C.—MARLOWE'S DEFECTS AS A DRAMATIST.

1. Want of humour.
2. Caring only for heroic types of character.
3. Inability to subordinate his poetic powers to the requirements of dramatic art.

Marlowe, in spite of his services to English drama, must be regarded greater as poet than dramatist.

QUESTIONS.

1. Compare the character of Marlowe's work with his life.
2. Give a history of blank verse before Marlowe; how far may Marlowe be said to have created this form of verse as an instrument of the drama?
3. Marlowe "first inspired with true poetic passion, the form of literature to which his chief efforts were consecrated." Show the truth of this statement.

The best edition of Marlowe's works is that edited by Bullen (A. H.), 3 vols. A cheap edition has recently been published in the Mermaid Series (price 2s. 6d.).

LECTURE VII.

MARLOWE AND HIS CIRCLE.

Greene, Peele, Lodge, and Nash, like Marlowe, were University playwrights in sympathy with, and writing for, the popular stage. The appearance of Tamberlaine marked a crisis in the literary life of each. Of the group, whom contemporary writers linked together, *Greene is most important as holding the same relation to Romantic Comedy as Marlowe does to Tragedy and History*.

A.—NASH AND LODGE

Hold a minor place among the Pre-Shakespearian playwrights, though both were eminent men of letters in their day—Nash as a satirist, Lodge as a writer of novels (notably "Rosalynde,' the source of "As You Like It").

i. NASH.

(*a*) His sole remaining play is *Will Summer's Testament*, a *Court* comedy, or "show" of the seasons. This dramatist had a hand in Marlowe's *Dido.* A lost play, the *Isle of Dogs*, is referred to by contemporary writers as having got the author into trouble, probably being a political libel.

(*b*) Especially important from a historical point of view is his address "To the Gentlemen Students of both Universities," prefixed to Greene's *Menaphon* (1589):—

e.g. "It is a common practise now a daies amongst a sort of shifting companions, that runne through euery arte and thrive by none, to leave the trade of *Nouerint* whereto they were borne, and busie themselves with the indeuors of Art, that could scarcelie latinize their necke-verse if they should have neede; yet English *Seneca* read by candle light yeeldes manie good sentences, *Bloud is a Begger*, and so forth; and if you intreate him faire in a frosty morning, he will afford you whole *Hamlets*, I should say handfulls of tragical speeches," etc.

ii. LODGE
- (a) Fought the cause of the drama against Gosson's *School of Abuse*, in "*A Defence of Poetry, Music, and Stageplays.*" Of this, in his "Alarum against Usurers," he wrote, "By reason of the slenderness of the subject (because it was in defence of plaies and playmakers), the godly and reverent, that had to deal in the cause, misliking it, forbad the publishing." Gosson framed his reply "Plays confuted in Five Actions," on a "private imperfect coppye."
- (b) As a playwright he helped Greene in *The Looking Glasse for London*, and wrote *The Wounds of Civil War lively set forth in the true Tragedies of Marius and Sulla*. The latter for the most part follows Tamberlaine, but is marred by—
    - i. Too many "jigging veins of rhyming mother wit."
    - ii. Too much clownage.
    - iii. An allegorical figure "Genius."
    - iv. Echo verses: a euphuistic conceit altogether non-Marlowesque.

B.—PEELE.
- (a) Though regarded rightly by his contemporaries as a greater poet than Greene, Peele holds no such important place as the latter in the history of the drama. He was no innovator, and thus forms no link in the development of the Elizabethan drama.
    1. His plays may be thus arranged:—
        - i. Pre-Tamberlaine plays:—
            The Arraignment of Paris (1584): A court allegorical, classical "show," rather than a "play"; written in rhyme (with one long blank verse passage).
            Sir Clyomon and Sir Clamydes (1584): In long rhyming couplets; the transition from the "vice" of the Moralities to the Shakespearian fool well illustrated by the comic character of "Subtle Shift."
        - ii. Marlowesque plays:—
            The Battle of Alcazar (acted in 1591), modelled on *Tamberlaine*.
            Edward I. (1593) due to the influence of *Edward II.* (but perhaps it preceded Marlowe's play).

Note in *The Battle of Alcazar*, the Presenter, who speaks Prologue before each act, the use of dumb shows, the introduction, as "dramatis personæ," of Jonas and Hercules.

 iii. Plays suggestive of revived early English drama:—
  (*a*) Interlude play: *Old Wives' Tale* (before 1595).
  (*b*) Miracle play: *David and Bathsheba* (before 1598).

2. Peele's chief characteristics:—
 1. The sweetness of his verse and diction.
 2. His want of humour.
 3. His dramas may best be described as "languid"—they lack energy and vigour.

C.—GREENE.

1. Specially noteworthy is the *autobiographical* character of some of his prose pieces, *e.g.*, *Never too Late*, *Groatsworth of Wit*, *Repentance*. From these may be inferred:—
 (*a*) His dramatic writings before 1586 (the date of the appearance of Tamberlaine) were not as successful as his novels.
 (*b*) His attitude towards Marlowe's innovations, especially his popularising of blank verse, was at first hostile: Greene's early attempts at blank verse met only with ridicule from his contemporaries.
 (*c*) His forced acceptance of Marlowe as his model.

2. Greene's plays may be divided into two periods:—
 (*a*) First period: Marlowesque plays:—
  i. In rivalry with *Tamberlaine*:—*Alphonsus* (but note the Choruses, Venus, and the Muses); *Orlando*.
  ii. In rivalry with *Faustus*:—*Friar Bacon* and *Friar Bungay*.
 (*b*) Second period: his later plays are marked by greater purity of diction, freedom from classicism, the use of blank verse, rhyme, and prose:—
  i. *James IV.*: only historical in dramatis personæ, remarkable as having acted prologue, fairy machinery, and interplay.
  ii. *George-à-Green*: a play of English country life, in which kings and rustics are commingled.

(*The Looking Glass for England*, written in conjunction with Lodge, may be described as a "miracle" with "interludes.")

D.— Greene's "Friar Bacon" and Marlowe's "Faustus."

The difference in the geniuses of the two dramatists and the essential characteristics of Greene's style may best be seen by a comparison of these two plays.

Note :—(*a*) The tragic ending of Marlowe's plays as contrasted with the happy ending of Greene's (all his plays are "*comical*").

(*b*) The "heroic" element in the Marlowan; the romantic in the Greenish drama.

(*c*) Greene possesses the humour that Marlowe lacks.

(*d*) Love used as motive in Greene; never in Marlowe. The finest types of womanhood in the pre-Shakesperian drama are to be found in Greene's plays.

(*e*) The freshness and buoyancy of English life give Greene's plays a charm altogether non-existent in the contemporary English drama.

(*f*) Marlowe, essentially a tragic poet, exhibits a psychological analysis of character; Greene, essentially a novelist, draws his characters as he finds them in the popular chap-books.

(*g*) Greene, as a novel-writer, is the first English dramatist who at all succeeds in blending different stories into a single play, though the blending is for the most part unsatisfactory.

Questions.

Attempt only question 3 or questions 1 and 2.

1. Give a short account of the influence of Marlowe's *Tamberlaine* on the contemporary dramatists.
2. Marlowe banished from the drama incongruous machinery standing outside the main action of plays. His avowed imitators could not succeed in this respect. Discuss the point.
3. Write an essay on Greene's *Friar Bacon* as compared with Marlowe's *Faustus*.

Professor Ward has edited Greene's *Friar Bacon* and Marlowe's *Faustus* for the Clarendon Press (price 6s.).

The best edition of the plays and poems of Greene and Peele is that edited by Dyce (Routledge, price 7s. 6d.).

LECTURE VIII.

SHAKESPEARE: FROM STRATFORD TO LONDON.

1.—SHAKESPEARE AT STRATFORD, 1564—1587.
    April 1564.—Born at Stratford-on-Avon. It is to be noted that Warwickshire, the county of the poet's birth, is situated in the centre of England, where the Celtic and Teutonic elements of the nation were most commingled.
    1582.—Shakespeare marries Anna Hathaway, who was eight years older than her husband.
    1587.—He leaves for London, and becomes connected with the theatre.

2.—EARLY YEARS IN LONDON.
    1592.—Robert Greene attacks Shakespeare in his *Groatsworth of Wit bought with a Million of Repentance.* After addressing Marlowe, Peele, and Nash, against trusting players, he adds:—"Yes, trust them not; for there is an upstart crow, beautified with our feathers, that with his *tyger's heart wrapt in a player's hide,* supposes he is as well able to bumbast out a blank verse as the best of you; and being an absolute *Johannes Factotum,* is in his owne conceit the onely Shake-scene in a country."

        This proof of Shakespeare's pre-eminence as a player and dramatist was followed a few months after by evidence of his worth as a man. Chettle apologised in December, 1592, for Greene's attack published by him:—"Myselfe have seene his demeanour no lesse civill, than he exelent in the qualitie he professes; besides, divers of worship have reported his uprightness of dealing, etc." N.B.—Shakespeare's dedication of *Venus and Adonis* (1593) and *Lucrece* (1594) to the Earl of Southampton.

The literary history circling round Greene's *Groatsworth of Wit,* tells the story of the contest between the player-poets *versus* scholar-poets. With this should be compared—
    i. The closing lines of Marlowe's first sestiad of *Hero and Leander*: "And but that Learning in despite of fate," etc. (about 1591).
    ii. Spenser's *Tears of the Muses* (1590).

3.—The chronology of these and of Shakespeare's plays generally, is determined more or less accurately by the following tests:—
    (*a*) EXTERNAL.
        i. Mention of Shakespeare's plays in other works.
        ii. Quotations from them in other works.
        iii. Entries at Stationers' Hall, etc.
    (*b*) INTERNAL.
        i. Quasi-external.
          e.g. 1. Allusions to passing events.
             2. Quotations from, or references to, other works.
        ii. Style.
          1. Use of prose and verse.
          2. Classical allusions.
          3. Puns, conceits.
          4. Thoughts "drawn" out and "packed."
        iii. Versification.
          1. Rhyme: rhymed heroics, doggerel, alternates, sonnet, or modified sonnet; use of couplets.
          2. End pause.
          3. Weak endings, light endings.
          4. Feminine ending.
        iv. Mental tests.
          1. Development of plot.
          2. Development of character.
          3. Use of certain characters.
          4. General considerations of the play as a whole.

4.—The chief external evidence for Shakespeare's early plays is Meres' list in his *Palladis Tamia*, or *Wit's Treasury* (1598). For the purposes of this course it will be sufficient to determine the order of these plays.

5.—i. Meres' list of Shakespeare's early plays is peculiarly important as a landmark: the date of its publication, 1598, was identical with the close of Shakespeare's earlier work, and the beginning of his more matured style.
    ii. The following grouping of the plays is probably in the main correct:—
        1587-89.—*Titus Andronicus.*
        1589-90.—*Love's Labour's Lost.*
            Love's Labour's Wonne (? *Taming of the Shrew*, or *All's well that Ends well*).

1589-90.—*Comedy of Errors.*
Two Gentlemen of Verona.
1591-93.—*Midsummer Night's Dream* (?).
Romeo and Juliet (revised later).
1593-94.—*Richard III.*
Richard II.
John.
1594-95.—*Midsummer Night's Dream* (?).
Romeo and Juliet (revised form).
1596-97.—*Merchant of Venice.*
Henry IV.

iii. Without insisting too strongly on the years affixed, this grouping of the plays is singularly suggestive.

Titus Andronicus must be regarded as anomalous and belonging to Shakespeare's apprentice years, and as standing outside the regular Shakespearian plays.

The three parts of *Henry VI.* (not mentioned by Meres) present special difficulties; 2 *Henry VI.*, and 3 *Henry VI.* being evidently revisions of earlier plays :—*The Contention* and *The True Tragedy :* in these revisions Shakespeare was assisted possibly by Marlowe, whose hand is clearly discernible in the old plays.

iv. *Titus Andronicus :—*

This play, *if studied at all,* must be taken in connection with Kyd's *Spanish Tragedy;* it is a mistake to describe it as Marlowan in anything but diction and versification. Shakespeare' contemporaries invariably classed it with Kyd's plays. It is probably an old play revised by the poet.

(The old play of *Hamlet*, from which Shakespeare probably took the subject of his tragedy, was, without much doubt, Kydian in subject and construction.)

cp. the machinery of the *Spanish Tragedy* and *Hamlet.*

QUESTIONS.

1. Discuss Greene's attack on Shakespeare
2. Explain the tests applied in attempting to settle the chronology of Shakespeare's plays.

3. Contrast Shakespeare's personal life with that of his contemporaries.

On chronology of Shakespeare's plays, see Dowden's "Shakespeare Primer" (1s.). The most thorough investigation of the subject is by H. P. Stokes, "An attempt to determine the chronological order of Shakespeare's plays" (Macmillan, 4s. 6d.).

For all the known facts connected with Shakespeare's life, see Halliwell's "Outlines of the Life of Shakespeare." Edition after edition is published by the author embodying the latest discoveries. The last edition published this year, (2 vols., Longmans & Co., 10s. 6d.).

Books on Shakespeare's dramatic art :—
    Gervinus : "Shakespeare Commentaries."
    Dowden : "Shakespeare : his Mind and Art."
    Moulton : "Shakespeare as a Dramatic Artist."

(These books are only mentioned as books of reference ; Dowden's "Shakespeare Primer" is sufficient guide. Students had best get on with the reading of the special plays, and not trouble too much with books about Shakespeare.

Read carefully (1) Love's Labour's Lost ;
             (2) Richard II. ;
             (3) Romeo and Juliet.)

LECTURE IX.

SHAKESPEARE'S EARLY COMEDIES.

A.—General Characteristics of these Plays.

    Shakespeare's first experiments in original dramatic composition, consisted in a series of comedies, "love-plays," marked by a strong family likeness and by distinct characteristics. The chief of these are (*see* Dowden's "Shakespeare : his Mind and Art," chap. 2) :—

i. *Versification* (Pre-Marlowan) :—
    (*a*) Fondness for rhyme, whether—
        (*aa*) Rhymed couplets; or
        (*bb*) Rhymed quatrains; or
        (*cc*) Alternate rhymes; or
        (*dd*) Doggerel.
    (*b*) Comparative absence of—
        (*aa*) Feminine endings.
        (*bb*) Weak endings.
        (*cc*) Unstopped lines.

(c) Regular structure of blank verse (*i.e.* absence of extra syllables, etc.).
ii. *Diction* :—
   (a) Many classical allusions occur.
   (b) Quibbles and conceits are frequent.
iii. *Imagery* :—Too elaborate and wordy.
iv. *Machinery* :—
   (a) Clowns, standing comparatively outside the main action.
   (b) Women of masculine nature : " termagant and shrewish."
v. Arrangement of characters almost geometrical.
vi. Want of ease in the evolution of plots : hence the explanatory tone of some of the soliloquies.

B.—GENERAL SURVEY OF THE EARLY COMEDIES, IN ALL OF WHICH " LOVE " ADVENTURES FORM THE CENTRAL POINT.

Love's Labour's Lost, a *topical* Elizabethan drama of *dialogue* and *satire*.

The Two Gentlemen of Verona.—Dramatisation of a romantic love story.

The Comedy of Errors.—A farce modelled on Latin comedy; a comedy of *incident*.

The Taming of the Shrew.

A comedy of *plot and character*. It is probable that *The Taming of the Shrew* belongs to this early period, and is mentioned in Meres' list under *Love's Labour's Wonne.* The play bears a strong likeness to *The Comedy of Errors*, especially in its long doggerel lines and language of the pre-Shakespearean drama. Compare the induction in this play with that of the old play of the *Taming of a Shrew* to understand the difference between Shakespeare's diction and the classical pedantry of the scholar poets and their imitators.

C.—LOVE'S LABOUR'S LOST.

Its topical character :—First ingeniously pointed out and elaborated by Mr. Sidney L. Lee (*see* " Gentleman's Magazine," 1880).

(a) Main element of the play refers to English volunteers, who, under Essex, had just joined *Navarre*, in France. Note the name of the hero of the play : his associates are named after Navarre's Generals. The mock earnestness with which the dramatist bids them repress their gaieties, and examine life in its severe aspects, burlesques "the frivolous sports and pastimes" with which it was known these officers passed away the intervals of warfare.

(*b*) References to Russian diplomacy with England.
(*c*) The question of academies.
(*d*) Contemporary affectations of speech and dress.
(*e*) "The ludicrous side of contemporary country life, with its inefficient constable, its pompous schoolmaster, and its ignorant curate."

D.—IN THESE EARLY COMEDIES SHAKESPEARE SEEMS MORE ESPECIALLY UNDER THE INFLUENCE OF GREENE, WHOM HE RESEMBLES IN—
1. His women characters.
2. His clowns.
3. Versification and diction, and prose dialogue.

This is especially true of *Midsummer Night's Dream*, which recalls Greene's *James IV*. The play probably owes its "lyrical and almost operatic tone, and masque-like form," to the fact of its having been written for some festivity or marriage.

QUESTIONS.

1. Point out elements in the early plays which connect themselves with the pre-Shakesperian drama.
2. Illustrate, from *Love's Labour's Lost*, the essential characteristics of Shakespeare's early plays.
3. Dwell on the contemporary affectations of speech satirised in *Love's Labour's Lost*.

LECTURE X.

SHAKESPEARE'S EARLY HISTORY PLAYS.

While Marlowe was alive Shakespeare wrote romantic comedies. He seems to have avoided anything like rivalry with his great contemporary until, after his death in 1593, he attempts—

(A.) A Marlowan play of the *Tamberlaine* type in *Richard III*.
(B.) A history play on the model of *Edward II.* in *Richard II*.

A.—RICHARD III.

1. In considering the influence of Marlowe on this play it must be borne in mind that Shakespeare had probably been working with Marlowe on 2 *Henry VI.* and 3 *Henry VI.*
2. The play naturally belongs to his group of history plays dealing with the House of York.
3. Marlowesque characteristics—
    (*a*) Richard, like Tamberlaine, or Faustus or Barabas, monopolises the whole action of the drama.
    (*b*) All the characters of this play of passion seem intended merely to set off the hero's "ideal villany."
    (*c*) The absence of evolution of character in the hero.
    (*d*) The hero's consciousness and avowal of his villany.
    (*e*) The tone of the play is often rather lyrical or epical than dramatic; *e.g.*, the lamentations of the women (Act ii., Sc. 2.; Act iv., Sc. 1).
    (*f*) Blank verse almost throughout: absence of prose, and of the general metrical forms found in the earlier plays.
4. In one respect at least, Shakespeare shows that he was no blind imitator of Marlowe: unlike him, he weaves Nemesis into the play and shows its consummation in Richard's fall.
5. The ghost machinery of the play, borrowed from the old play of the *True Tragedy of Richard III.*
6. Early plays on the subject—
    (1) *Richardus Tertius*, acted at Cambridge in 1583.
    (2) Churchyard's *Challenge*, including the *Tragedie of Shore's Wife*, 1593.
    (3) The *True Tragedie of Richard III.*, 1593.
7. The extraordinary difference between the quartos of this play (1597-1598) and the text of the first folio can only be accounted for by regarding the latter as due to a revision of the former.

B.—RICHARD II.

1. Shakespeare having completed the York series of plays by *Richard III.*, probably then wrote *Richard II.* as an introduction to the Lancastrian plays.
2. There can be no doubt that this play was suggested by Marlowe's *Edward II.*: it holds the same relation to *Richard III.* as Marlowe's play does to his earlier typical tragedies: like it
    (1.) It is pitched in a lower key than *Richard III.*, and

      (2.) Shows greater power of characterisation; Richard II. does not stand alone in the play.

      (3.) Special scenes in *Edward II.*, especially the deposition scene, served as models to Shakespeare in parallel scenes in this play.

3, As regards versification, it is to be noted that Shakespeare broke away from Marlowan models—

      (1.) One-fifth of the play is in rhyme.

      (2.) Noteworthy is, however, the fact that these rhyming passages abound in the early parts of the play, and that the most powerful speeches are entirely in blank verse.

      (3.) The absence of prose in this play, as in *Richard III*, is due to Marlowe's example.

4. Several plays contemporary or anterior treated the same subject. Daniel's poem *Civil Wars* (2nd edition, 1595) either suggested points to Shakespeare or *vice versâ*.

5. The deposition scene was not printed till 1608. It was probably not acted, and suppressed in the edition of 1597, in consequence of a papal bull issued against the Queen, in 1596, inciting her subjects to rebellion. In 1599 Hayward was imprisoned for publishing his *History of the First Year of Henry IV.*, *i.e.*, the story of the deposition of Richard II.

C.—KING JOHN.

1. This play must be compared with the old play, the *Troublesome Raygne of King John*, on which it is founded, to understand Shakespeare's dramatic touch at this early period.

2. The old "two-sectioned" play may be described as the work of an imitator of Marlowe clinging to pre-Marlowan versification and diction and clownage.

3. Shakespeare, in his handling of the old play leaves the incidents nearly the same (the most important omission being a comic doggerel farce satirising monastic life), but touches the characters with new life.

4. In *King John*, Shakespeare makes an advance on *Richard II.*, and all his previous plays in the large proportion of blank verse lines; like *Richard II*, no place is given in it to prose.

QUESTIONS.

1. Give a short sketch of the pre-Shakespearian drama, dealing with

national history. Distinguish carefully a "chronicle history" from a "historical drama."
2. How far would it be right to argue from metrical tests the priority in composition of *Richard II.* or *Richard III.?*
3. Write a short essay on Charles Lamb's criticism :—"The reluctant pangs of abdicating royalty in *Edward II.* furnished hints which Shakespeare scarcely improved in his *Richard II.*"

LECTURE XI.

ROMEO AND JULIET.

"In our opinion the same features as in *Romeo and Juliet* may be recognised in the three most celebrated stories of all time : 'Hero and Leander,' 'Pyramus and Thisbe,' among the ancients, and 'Tristan and Isolde' among the moderns."—(*Simrock*.)

1. Shakespeare's earliest tragedy is ranged on the same bases as his early comedies, *i.e.*, romantic love. The Marlowan tragedy seems to have had no attractions for him; the Kydian "tragedy of the shambles," *Titus Andronicus*, is clearly outside Shakespeare's early regular drama. Later on, when he left the tragedy of "love passion," and wrote his tragedy of introspection, *Hamlet*, based on the Kydian type of tragedy, he had already formed his mature style.
2. The Story :—
    (1) The main elements of the story have been traced as far back as to Greek medieval writers of the fifth century; but the story became localised in Italy, the Veronese fixing the date of the tragedy in the year 1303.
    (2) Dante, reproaching the Emperor Albert for neglect of Italy, wrote :—
        Come, see the Capulets and Montagues,
        The Filippeschi and Monaldi, man,
        Who car'st for nought! Those sunk in grief, and these
        With dire suspicion rack'd.
    (3) To this day the Veronese show the site and relics of the lovers' grave.

(4) Although several earlier stories exist recalling that of Romeo and Juliet, these names of the lovers are not found before 1535 in Italian literature, when the history of Romeo and Juliet was told by Luigi da Porto ("La Giuletta," 1535).

(5) After this several versions were made of the story. Most important is that of Bandello (1554), and this, with that writer's other novels, passed into French in 1559.

(6) English versions:—
　　i. Arthur Brooke's:—"*The Tragicall Hystorye of Romeo and Juliet*, written first in Italian by Bandell, and nowe in Englishe by Ar. Br."
　　ii. Paynter's novel:—"*The goodly history of the true and constant love between Rhomeo and Julietta, the one of whom died of poyson, the other of sorrow and hevinesse: wherein be comprised many adventures of love, and other devises touchinge the same* (1567, in the "Palace of Pleasure"); due to the French rendering of Bandello's novel in Boisteau's "Histoires Tragiques."

(7) Shakespeare, though there is no doubt that he was acquainted with both these versions, followed Brooke's poem; though it must be remembered that, according to Brooke's statement, an old English play on the subject also existed.

(8) Shakespeare closely follows the poem, and the play betrays its influence on its diction. The poem abounds in conceits and antitheses, which may be paralleled with instances from the play.

(9) The "argument" of Brooke's poem will serve to show how nearly the dramatist follows it as regards plot:—

> Love hath inflamed twayne by sodayn sight,
> And both do graunt the thing that both desyre;
> They wed in shrift by counsell of a frier;
> Yong Romeus clymes fayre Juliet's bower by night,
> Three months he doth enioy his cheefe delight:
> By Tybalt's rage, provoked unto yre,
> He payeth death to Tybalt for his hyre.
> A banisht man, he 'scapes by secret flight:

>New mariage is offred to his wife:
>She drinkes a drinke that seemes to reve her breath:
>They bury her, that sleping yet hath lyfe.
>Her husband heares the tydinges of her death;
>He drinkes his bane; and she, with Romeus' knyfe,
>When she awakes, her selfe alas she sleath.

(10) Shakespeare shows his dramatic skill in dealing with the poem:—
- i. By compressing the action, which in the story occupies four or five months, to within as many days.
- ii. He re-creates the character of Mercutio, in the poem a mere "courtier," "bold among the bashful maydes."
- iii. In making Paris die at the grave of Juliet by the hand of Romeo: in the poem nothing is heard of the Count after his disappointment.

(11) But one is only able to say that in subject Shakespeare followed Brooke, in its *spirit* the play transcends altogether the poem.

"With Brooke, all is the play of fortune, chance, destiny; a touching story of two lovers subjected to an alternation of prosperity and misfortune. But with Shakespeare the piece is the necessary history of *all* strong *love*, which in itself deep, true, and living, is not guided and effected by any external influence, but which rises superior to every other passion and emotion, beating proudly against the barriers of conventionality, occupied to excess alone with itself and its satisfaction, deriding the representations of cold discretion: aye, over bold, defying fate itself, and neglecting its warnings to its own ruin."— (*Gervinus.*)

(12) Characteristics of *Romeo and Juliet* as an early work:—
- i. Frequency of rhymes.
- ii. Sonnet form.
- iii. Conceits, alliteration.
- iv. Its lyrical character (partly due to nature of the subject).

(13) In 1597 a quarto edition of the play first published; this was without much doubt a mutilated printed copy of the play in its early form, an improved and revised version of which was issued in 1599.

QUESTIONS.

1. Brooke mentions an early play on *Romeo and Juliet* before 1562. Attempt a rough description of this lost play in order to illustrate the advance in dramatic art between its appearance and Shakespeare's plays.
2. "Local colour" is almost unknown in the English drama before *Romeo and Juliet*: discuss this.
3. Explain from *Romeo and Julzet* the state in which the earlier printed plays of Shakespeare have come down to us.

LECTURE XII.

RETROSPECTIVE AND PROSPECTIVE.

1. RETROSPECTIVE SURVEY :—
    Shakespeare's relation to (*a*) the early English drama,
    (*b*) his contemporaries.

    The series of Shakespearian plays treated may be described as the poet's experiments in search of the dramatic form best suited to his genius.

    Romeo and Juliet established the poet's reputation and called forth from university men an avowal of the triumph of the player poets over the scholar poets.—(*See* "Pilgrimage to Parnassus," 1598.)

    Hamlet had not yet appeared when a university pen wrote :—
    "Few of the university pen plaies well, they smell too much of that writer Ovid and that writer Metamorphosis, and talke too much of Proserpina and Suppiter. *Why, here's our fellow Shakespeare puts them all downe,*" etc.— ("Return from Parnassus," 1601.)

2. PROSPECTIVE GLANCE FORWARD INTO THE HISTORY OF THE SHAKESPEARIAN DRAMA AND THE ELIZABETHAN-JACOBITE DRAMA GENERALLY.

CPSIA information can be obtained
at www.ICGtesting.com
Printed in the USA
BVHW090124211118
533638BV00012B/932/P

9 781330 518656